THE RETIREMENT GAME PLAYBOOK

Level Up, Unlock Perks, and Conquer Your Fears, You're Not Alone

By Sarai Del Mar

Published with the wisdom and guidance of Sean O'Leary Books LL

AF720503

Visit www.seanolearybooks.com for more books by Sarai Del Mar

Legal Disclaimer:

This book is a work of fiction. Any similarities to real persons, living or dead, are purely coincidental.

No AI apps were harmed in the making of this book.

Maybe some nudging, but the concept, direction, style and tone were all the author's doing.

SEAN O'LEARY BOOKS

READ TO BELIEVE

Published with the wisdom and guidance of Sean O'Leary Books LLC

Visit www.seanolearybooks.com for more books by Sarai De Ma

Prologue: The Game of Life and the Art of Retirement

Mickey Castillo had spent forty years making all the "right" moves—steady job, steady paycheck, steady climb up the corporate ladder. He was a king on the chessboard of life, dodging pawns, capturing promotions, and sacrificing a weekend here, a vacation there, all in pursuit of the ultimate checkmate: a comfortable, worry-free retirement.

And now?

Now, at sixty-four, with a retirement seminar brochure in one hand and a decaf coffee in the other, he was beginning to suspect he'd been playing the wrong game all along.

Chess? Please. Retirement wasn't chess. Retirement was poker.

✅ You bet on Social Security.
✅ You bluffed your way through stock market swings.
✅ You folded on the McMansion and downsized to something reasonable.

And if you played your cards right, you didn't end up scratching lottery tickets for groceries by seventy-five.

Mickey wasn't ready to go all in just yet.

So, like any good strategist facing a mid-game crisis, he called in reinforcements.

Which is how he found himself at The Last Round, a cozy, dimly lit café-bar where:

✅ The booths were comfortable
✅ The drinks were strong
✅ And the coffee was even stronger.

The bartender, Tony, had perfected the art of listening without contributing, making it the perfect spot for overthinkers, schemers, and anyone staring down the barrel of financial ruin.

Across the table sat his four closest friends—all at different points on the retirement spectrum, all equally bewildered by this "next phase of life" nonsense.

Meet The Retirement Club:

Penelope Dixon (62) – The Budget Queen.
A retired schoolteacher with a PhD in stretching a dollar. Give her twenty bucks, and she'd return with a week's worth of groceries, a fully stamped coffee loyalty card, and a free muffin—just because she "charmed" the barista. She still saved every receipt, "just in case."

Jason "JJ" Cortez (60) – The Late Bloomer.
Former owner of *Cortez's Mobile Tacos*, a food truck that never quite turned into the empire he'd imagined. He had passion, enthusiasm, and absolutely no savings. His current financial strategy involved manifesting money and "waiting for crypto to come back."

Winnie "Niecy" Hu (59) – The Side Hustle Strategist.
A former HR executive who believed that retirement was just a state of mind. She was semi-retired, fully caffeinated, and still juggling consulting gigs, rental properties, and an Etsy store where she sold homemade planners for "overwhelmed professionals." She'd read every finance book ever written and color-coded her retirement plan.

Carson Templ (58) – The Gambler.
A former stockbroker turned “market strategist,” which was a fancy way of saying he still traded stocks while wearing pajamas. He claimed he could beat the system, but he also once lost half his savings on an investment in artisanal goat cheese futures. He believed the secret to a wealthy retirement was "risk, reward, and a good gut feeling."

Together, they made up The Retirement Club—not by choice, but by necessity.

Because if they were going to survive the next twenty, thirty, or goodness help them, forty years…

They had better start figuring out the rules of the game.

And fast.

Chapter 1: The Retirement Game Begins

Mickey adjusted his reading glasses and studied the retirement checklist he had printed from the internet.

✔ Savings? ☑ (Mostly. Let's not talk about that one bad real estate deal.)
✔ Investments? ☑ (If we ignore that stock tip from Carson.)
✔ Social Security? ❓ (Pending investigation.)
✔ Clear plan? ❌ (Highly debatable.)

He sighed and looked up at his friends.

"Alright," he said. "Tell me something. If retirement is a game… what kind of game is it?"

Penelope sipped her tea, her coupon-stuffed purse perched beside her like a loyal pet.

"It's like a board game," she said. "You save, strategize, and if you play well, you get to pass Go and actually enjoy yourself."

JJ leaned forward, tapping his fingers against the table.

"Nah, it's more like a video game. Boss fights, side quests, and surprise level-ups when you realize you qualify for a senior discount."

Winnie scoffed.

"It's a spreadsheet," she said. "A giant, terrifying spreadsheet. With color-coded categories and absolutely no undo button."

Carson smirked, flipping a poker chip between his fingers.

"It's blackjack," he said. "You make your bets, hope the dealer doesn't screw you, and try not to go bust before you hit seventy."

Mickey exhaled.

Well, that was helpful.

"Okay," he said. "But how do you win?"

They exchanged glances.

JJ shrugged. "You don't end up broke?"

Winnie rolled her eyes. "You get to live how you want?"

Penelope smiled. "You retire with dignity?"

Carson cracked his knuckles. "You beat the system."

Mickey let their answers settle.

That was the thing about games—you had to know the goal before you could make a winning strategy.

He tapped the table.

"Alright, then. We need a plan. A real one."

JJ leaned back. "What, like a rulebook?"

"Yes," Mickey said. "A Retirement Rulebook. Something simple. Something that works."

Penelope nodded. "And something that doesn't involve eating cat food at eighty."

Mickey grabbed a napkin and scrawled across it:

✓ THE RETIREMENT GAME: HOW TO WIN.

Then he looked around the table.

This was it. The opening move.

Because retirement wasn't something that happened to you.

It was a game.

And if they played it right?

They were going to win.

Chapter 2: The Crossroads: Traveling vs. Settling Down

Mickey barely had time to take a sip of his coffee before a new voice joined the conversation.

"I need help."

The table turned to see a tall, slightly frazzled man in his early sixties—gray hair, pressed khakis, and the unmistakable look of a man standing at the edge of a major life decision.

"Retirement emergency?" JJ guessed.

The man nodded. "You could say that. I'm Thomas. I just retired last month, and now I have no idea what I'm supposed to do."

"Welcome to the club," Carson said.

Thomas pulled out a pamphlet from his pocket and dropped it on the table. The title read:

✅ "Retirement: The World Is Your Oyster!"

The Retirement Club collectively grimaced.

"I thought I'd spend my retirement traveling, you know?" Thomas said. "Seeing the world. Italy, Thailand, maybe even Antarctica if I get bored. But now? I don't know. The idea of living out of a suitcase suddenly feels exhausting."

"Ah," Penelope said, nodding. "The 'travel vs. settle down' dilemma."

Thomas sighed. "I spent my whole life dreaming about seeing the world. Now that I can, I don't know if I want to. Am I… failing at retirement?"

Mickey chuckled. "No, you're just realizing something most people don't figure out until it's too late."

"What's that?" Thomas asked.

"Retirement isn't a vacation."

The Debate: Travel vs. Stability

"Alright," Mickey said. "Let's break this down. Two retirement paths."

✅ Path One: The Nomad Life. Travel, adventure, new experiences.
✅ Path Two: The Settled Life. Stability, routine, a place to call home.

"Which one's better?" Thomas asked.

"Depends on the person," Penelope said, flipping open her notebook of wisdom.

✅ TRAVEL: Pros & Cons

✅ **Pros**:

- Endless adventure and new experiences.
- More flexibility—you can adjust your lifestyle to match your budget.
- The thrill of waking up somewhere new.

❌ **Cons**:

- Expensive (and unpredictable).
- Medical care is trickier abroad.
- Living out of a suitcase gets old—fast.

✅ STAYING PUT: Pros & Cons

✅ **Pros**:

- Stable expenses and predictable costs.
- Access to healthcare, doctors, and a known support system.
- A consistent social life—neighbors, friends, community.

❌ **Cons**:

- Can feel repetitive or even boring.
- Harder to change gears if you get restless.
- Less spontaneous adventure.

Thomas leaned back in his chair. "Great. So basically, both options are good and bad. How do I choose?"

"You don't," Carson said, shrugging. "You do both."

The Hybrid Retirement Strategy

"Who says retirement has to be one thing or the other?" Carson continued.

"Yeah," JJ added. "Why not travel part of the year and settle down the rest?"

Penelope nodded. "Or downsize your house and use the extra money for extended trips?"

"Or," Carson said, grinning, "you go full retirement hacker and house-sit for rich people in Europe."

Thomas blinked. "Wait, what?"

"Yeah, it's a thing," Carson said. "People let retirees house-sit luxury homes while they travel. Free rent, great views, and usually a cat to feed."

Thomas looked intrigued. "That's… actually brilliant."

Mickey tapped the table. "See? Retirement isn't about choosing one lifestyle and sticking to it forever. It's about knowing when to roll the dice and when to play it safe."

The Retirement Club's Second Rule

By the time Thomas left, he wasn't agonizing over his next move—he was making a flexible plan.

✅ A few months traveling.
✅ A stable home base.
✅ A plan to adjust when needed.

As he walked out the door, Mickey picked up his napkin of wisdom and scribbled down their newest rule:

✅ "Retirement isn't a destination—it's a strategy."

Carson looked over his shoulder. "That one's actually pretty good."

"Yeah," Mickey said. "And something tells me… we're gonna need more napkins."

Chapter 3: Timelines and Tactics: Mastering Retirement Ages

John sat at *The Last Round*, staring at his retirement projections like they were some kind of cruel prank.

"I thought I had this all figured out," he muttered, pushing the paper toward Mickey.

Mickey adjusted his reading glasses and took a look.

✅ Retire at 62? Smaller checks, more time to enjoy life.
✅ Wait until 67? Bigger checks, but five more years of work.
✅ Hold off until 70? Even bigger checks… but what if you don't make it that far?

John sighed. "So basically, I either live a little poorer now or risk waiting too long."

Carson smirked. "Yep. Retirement planning is one big, anxiety-filled guessing game."

"Fantastic," John muttered.

The Retirement Age Debate: Time vs. Money

"Alright," Mickey said, pulling out a napkin for another round of wisdom. "What's more valuable—time or money?"

John frowned. "Both?"

"Wrong answer," Penelope said, flipping open her infamous notebook.

✅ Retiring early (62-64)

☑️ **Pros**:

- More time for travel, hobbies, and naps.
- Escape the soul-sucking office life.
- If you’re in good health, you can enjoy your best years.

❌ **Cons**:

- Smaller Social Security checks forever.
- Need more savings to fill the gap.
- Medicare doesn’t kick in until 65, so health insurance is on you.

✅ Retiring at Full Retirement Age (65-67)

☑️ **Pros**:

- Full Social Security benefits.
- Medicare kicks in—huge win.
- Balances time and money better.

❌ **Cons**:

- More years working.
- Possibly less energy for adventure.
- Might start questioning your sanity at work.

✅ Retiring Late (70 and beyond)

☑️ **Pros**:

- Biggest Social Security payout (up to 32% more).
- More financial security.

- Less risk of outliving your money.

❌ **Cons**:

- Less time to actually enjoy retirement.
- Work burnout is real.
- The extra money won't mean much if you're too tired to use it.

The Poker Game of Retirement

John rubbed his temples. "So what's the right move?"

"There isn't one," Mickey said. "It's poker. You have to play the hand you're dealt."

"You bet on your health, your finances, and your best guess at the future."

John exhaled sharply. "So… there's no perfect answer?"

Penelope smiled. "Nope. Just a strategy that works for you."

The Hybrid Approach: The Real Retirement Cheat Code

Carson grinned. "Why not half-retire?"

John raised an eyebrow. "What do you mean?"

✅ Work part-time and claim Social Security later.
✅ Ease into retirement instead of jumping off a cliff.
✅ Consult, freelance, or side hustle for extra income.

JJ nodded. "Or cut expenses now so you don't need as much later."

John sat back. "So, I don't have to retire all at once?"

"Exactly," Mickey said, scribbling on his napkin.

✅ "Retirement isn't about when—it's about how."

John read the napkin, then smiled.

"Alright," he said. "I think I finally get it."

He folded the napkin and tucked it into his pocket.

And just like that?

He had a plan.

Chapter 4: The Holistic Retirement Blueprint

Penelope Dixon did not believe in half-baked plans.

She planned her meals, she planned her vacations, and—if given enough time—she could probably plan an apocalypse survival strategy complete with color-coded escape routes.

So, when she overheard yet another retiree at *The Last Round* saying, *"I have my 401(k), I'm all set,"* she nearly choked on her tea.

"Oh, honey," she muttered, shaking her head.

That's when she knew—The Retirement Club needed a wake-up call.

The Big Mistake: Thinking Retirement Is Just About Money

The usual crew had barely settled into their booth when Penelope slammed a massive binder onto the table.

Mickey, halfway through his coffee, jumped. "What the hell is that?"

"Your future," Penelope said.

JJ squinted at the bold title on the cover:

✔ The Holistic Retirement Blueprint: Because Finances Aren't Everything

Carson raised an eyebrow. "You mean there's more to retirement than not going broke?"

Penelope flipped open to page one.

✅ 1. Financial Stability – So you don't end up eating discount tuna at 80.
✅ 2. Health & Wellness – Because money means nothing if you're too sick to enjoy it.
✅ 3. Social Connections – To avoid becoming the neighborhood hermit.
✅ 4. Purpose & Passion – Because there's only so much daytime TV you can watch.

"You mean," JJ said, leaning in, "retirement isn't just about hoarding cash and waiting to die?"

"Nope," Penelope said. "It's about designing a life you actually want to live."

Step 1: Financial Stability (AKA: The Bare Minimum)

"Alright," Mickey said. "Let's start with the obvious. Money. How do we keep it long enough to enjoy it?"

✅ Make a spending plan. (Not a budget. Budgets are depressing.)
✅ Downsize or right-size. Because a mansion is just more rooms to clean.
✅ Stay invested. Your money needs to work harder than you do.
✅ Have an emergency fund. Life is unpredictable. Your bank account shouldn't be.

"If you get this part wrong," Carson said, grinning, "you're playing retirement on hard mode."

Step 2: Health & Wellness (AKA: What's the Point of Money If You're Too Sick to Enjoy It?)

"Here's what no one tells you," Penelope said, flipping to the next section. "If you don't plan for your health, your retirement will be nothing but doctor visits and medical bills."

✅ Move every day. Walk, dance, lift things—preferably not just the remote.
✅ Strength training. Muscles keep you from falling like a badly stacked Jenga tower.
✅ Nutrition matters. Not saying you need to eat kale, but maybe rethink the daily cheeseburgers.
✅ Get enough sleep. Or prepare for a future where you doze off in the middle of conversations.

"So, basically," JJ said, "don't turn into a rusty old car that breaks down every five miles."

"Exactly," Penelope said.

Step 3: Social Connections (AKA: How to Not Become a Lonely Weirdo)

"You know what's worse than running out of money?" Penelope asked.

"Running out of tequila?" Carson guessed.

"Running out of people," Penelope corrected.

✅ Keep a social routine. Meet friends for coffee. Join a group. Leave the house.
✅ Talk to someone daily. Even if it's just the barista at your favorite

café.
✅ Be intentional about friendships. Don't just wait for invitations—make them.
✅ Volunteer or mentor. It's scientifically proven to make you less grumpy.

"Basically," Penelope said, looking around the table, "if you want to avoid a sad, isolated retirement, stay connected."

"Or," JJ added, "get a dog."

"That too," Penelope agreed.

Step 4: Purpose & Passion (AKA: How to Not Become a Bored, Aimless Lump)

"Alright," Mickey said, folding his arms, "let's talk about the real problem. What do we actually do all day?"

Silence.

Then Carson sighed. "That's… a fair question."

✅ Find something new. A hobby, a skill, anything that stops you from binge-watching infomercials.
✅ Work (on your terms). Part-time, consulting, freelancing—not because you have to, but because you want to.
✅ Give back. Teach, mentor, volunteer—pass down your knowledge.
✅ Travel… but with a plan. Aimless wandering sounds fun until you realize you're just lost.

"You need a reason to get out of bed," Penelope said. "And Netflix isn't it."

The Retirement Club's Fourth Rule

By the time they wrapped up, The Retirement Club had a new rule:

✅ "Retirement isn't just about money—it's about life."

JJ leaned back. "Alright, I'll admit it. This might be the most important one yet."

Penelope smiled, satisfied. "See? Told you."

Mickey scribbled the rule onto his napkin of wisdom and nodded.

This wasn't just about surviving retirement.

This was about winning it.

Chapter 5: Starting Line: Breaking the Retirement Planning Myth

Thomas Castillo had always considered himself a responsible man.

He paid his bills on time. He followed financial advice columns like they were the gospel. And yet—here he was, sitting at *The Last Round*, gripping a lukewarm coffee, realizing that he had no actual plan for retirement.

"So," he said, exhaling sharply, "I think I screwed up."

The Retirement Club, midway through their Seniors Lunch Special, turned to him in unison.

"No plan?" Mickey guessed.

"Not enough saved?" Penelope offered.

"Crypto?" Carson asked, grinning.

Thomas groaned. "All of the above."

Silence.

Then Winnie clapped her hands together. "Good news! It's never too late to fix it."

Thomas blinked. "Are you sure? Because according to every retirement article I've read, I should have started planning in the womb."

"Yeah, yeah," Carson waved him off. "Ignore the scare tactics. Let's break this down."

And just like that, The Retirement Club turned their focus to a new mission:

Helping Thomas escape the "I'm screwed" mindset.

Step 1: Face the Numbers (AKA: Look at the Damage)

Penelope slid a blank notepad across the table.

"First rule of fixing retirement: stop ignoring your finances. Write it all down."

✅ How much do you have? (Even if it's a depressing number.)
✅ How much debt do you owe? (So you don't drag it into retirement.)
✅ What are your expenses? (Because those don't magically disappear.)

"Can I just… pretend everything's fine?" Thomas asked, half-joking.

"Nope," Penelope said. "We deal in facts, not feelings."

Step 2: Destroy Debt Like It Owes You Money

"You don't want to enter retirement still paying off past mistakes," JJ said.

✅ Credit cards? Gone.
✅ Car payments? Minimized.
✅ Random subscriptions? Canceled. (Seriously, why was Thomas still subscribed to *Gourmet Cat Weekly*?)

"Debt in retirement," Penelope said, "is like wearing ankle weights in a marathon. It slows you down and makes everything harder."

Thomas nodded, scribbling notes. "So, kill debt ASAP. Got it."

Step 3: Max Out Catch-Up Contributions (AKA: The IRS Actually Gives You Free Money—Take It)

"You're 62," Mickey said. "Which means you qualify for catch-up contributions."

Thomas tilted his head. "What now?"

"You can put an extra $7,500 per year into your 401(k) and $1,000 extra into an IRA."

"So… the government is letting me supercharge my savings?"

"Yep," Penelope confirmed. "And you should take full advantage."

Step 4: Delay Social Security (If Possible)

"Okay," Thomas said, rubbing his temples. "I always assumed I should take Social Security at 62."

"Bad move," Mickey said.

✔ Claim at 62? You get 75% of your full benefit.
✔ Wait until 67? You get 100%.
✔ Hold off until 70? You get 132%.

"So, the longer I wait, the bigger my check?"

"Exactly," Penelope said. "If you can afford to delay claiming, it pays off."

Step 5: Make Extra Money (Without Hating Your Life)

Thomas sighed. "So… I need to keep working?"

"Not necessarily," Carson said. "You need income. But that doesn't mean you have to stay in your old job."

✅ Consulting gigs?
✅ Freelance work?
✅ Side hustles that don't suck?

"Ever thought about teaching a class?" JJ asked.

Thomas paused. "Actually… I always wanted to. But I never had time."

"Well," Penelope smiled, "now you do."

The Retirement Club's Fifth Rule

Thomas sat back, staring at his scribbled notes.

"So you're saying… I'm not doomed?"

"Not if you start now," Penelope said.

Mickey scribbled onto his napkin of wisdom:

✅ "It's never too late to play smart."

Thomas took a deep breath and nodded.

"Alright," he said. "I think I just found my starting line."

And just like that, he had a plan.

Chapter 6: Game Mechanics: Understanding Retirement Topics

By now, The Retirement Club had covered a lot of ground—enough to turn their weekly lunches at The Last Round into something of a phenomenon.

Each week, more retirees showed up, pulled in by whispers of "those people who actually make retirement planning make sense"—or, as Carson called it, "the best unpaid consulting gig we never signed up for."

And today? Today was Game Mechanics Day.

"Alright," Mickey said, leaning back in his chair. "We've talked about what we want from retirement. Now let's talk about the rules of the game."

Penelope flipped open her notorious notebook. "You mean the complicated, confusing, and poorly explained rules that no one actually understands?"

"Exactly," Mickey said.

Carson smirked. "So, everything that keeps people up at night?"

"Yep," Mickey said. "Let's fix that."

Step 1: The Mystery of Retirement Accounts

"Show of hands," Mickey said. "Who here has multiple old retirement accounts they've never done anything with?"

A few hesitant hands went up.

"See?" Mickey said. "People collect 401(k)s like they're coffee mugs."

"So what do we do with them?" asked Thomas, still fresh from his retirement panic.

Penelope ticked off options on her fingers.

✅ Leave them where they are. (Not great.)
✅ Roll them into an IRA. (Better control, better investment options.)
✅ Consolidate into your current employer's plan. (If you're still working.)

"Bottom line?" Mickey said. "Money sitting in old accounts isn't working for you."

"Like a lazy roommate who never pays rent," JJ added.

"Exactly," Mickey said.

Step 2: The Social Security Puzzle

"Alright," Penelope said, flipping to a new section. "Who here actually understands how Social Security works?"

Silence.

"That's what I thought," she said.

✅ Claim at 62? Smaller checks, but you get money sooner.
✅ Wait until full retirement age (67 for most)? You get your full benefit.
✅ Hold off until 70? You get an 8% increase for each year you wait.

"So," JJ said, tilting his head, "if I wait, I get more money?"

"Yes," Penelope said. "But only if you can afford to wait. If you need the money sooner, taking it early isn't wrong—just strategic."

Step 3: The Healthcare Maze (AKA: How Not to Get Destroyed by Medical Bills)

"You know what's worse than getting old?" Stella, a new member, asked.

"Surprise medical bills?" JJ guessed.

"Ding, ding, ding," Stella said.

✔ Medicare Part A – Covers hospitals. (Usually free.)
✔ Medicare Part B – Covers doctor visits. (Costs money.)
✔ Medicare Part C (Advantage Plans) – Private insurance that bundles A & B.
✔ Medicare Part D – Covers prescriptions.

"And here's the thing," Stella said. "If you don't sign up at the right time, you get penalty fees for life."

"Wait—for life?!" Carl, another new attendee, looked horrified.

"Yep," Stella said. "Like a bad decision in Monopoly you can't take back."

Step 4: Investment Strategies for Retirement

"Alright," Carson said, shuffling a deck of playing cards. "Let's talk investments. Because if you're retired and still investing like a 30-year-old day trader… you're playing the game wrong."

✅ Too aggressive? You could lose too much.
✅ Too conservative? Your money won't keep up with inflation.
✅ Best strategy? Balanced investing—some safe, some growth-focused.

"Think of it like poker," Carson said. "You wanna stay in the game, but you don't wanna bet everything on one risky move."

The Senior Center Invitation

As the meeting wrapped up, another familiar face walked up—the senior center coordinator.

"You all ready for your first class next week?" she asked.

Mickey exchanged a look with the group. "Yeah. We're ready."

"Great," she said. "Because our biggest request? People want to know how to handle all the unexpected stuff that happens in retirement."

Carson grinned. "Well, they came to the right place."

Because if there was one thing The Retirement Club had mastered?

It was making things work—no matter what life threw at them.

Final Takeaway: Understanding the Game Mechanics of Retirement

✅ Retirement accounts? Make your money work for you.
✅ Social Security? Know when to claim strategically.

✅ Healthcare? Avoid Medicare landmines.
✅ Investments? Balance risk and security.

The Retirement Club had accidentally become retirement experts.

And now?

They were taking the game to a bigger stage.

Next stop: The Senior Center.

Chapter 7: Winning the Retirement Endgame: Estate Planning & Leaving a Legacy

By now, The Retirement Club had built a reputation—one they never planned on.

What started as five friends just trying to survive retirement had turned into standing-room-only meetups at The Last Round, packed with retirees who had heard about them through whispers of:

✅ "They actually explain this stuff without making me feel like an idiot."
✅ "They saved me from signing a terrible financial deal."
✅ "And they're funnier than my financial planner."

And today? Today's topic was the one no one wanted to talk about.

Estate Planning.

Otherwise known as: "What happens after you die, and how big of a mess are you leaving behind?"

Penelope set down her notebook. "Alright, let's get this out of the way."

"Let me guess," Carson said. "Everyone hates talking about estate planning?"

"Yep," Penelope said. "Because people think it's about death."

"Well… isn't it?" Carl, one of the newer attendees, asked.

"No," Penelope said. "It's about control. You're making sure your money, your property, and your wishes go where you want them to—without your family ending up in probate court for two years."

"Or fighting like contestants on a reality show," JJ added.

"Exactly," Penelope said. "And that's why we're going to make this as painless as possible."

Step 1: The Must-Have Documents

Penelope pulled out a checklist and held it up like a teacher about to assign homework.

✅ A Will – Says who gets what. If you don't have one? The state decides.
✅ Power of Attorney (POA) – Who handles your finances if you can't?
✅ Advance Healthcare Directive – Who makes medical decisions if you're unable?
✅ A Trust (If Needed) – Avoids probate, which is slow, expensive, and a nightmare.

"Let me guess," Mickey said. "Most people don't have these?"

"Correct," Penelope said. "And that's how you get family members brawling over an old recliner."

Step 2: Avoiding Probate Nightmares

"I had a friend," Miriam, a retired nurse, chimed in, "whose mother died without a will. What should've been a simple inheritance turned into a two-year legal battle."

Everyone winced.

"So," Penelope said, "if you want to avoid that disaster:"

✅ Make a will or trust. (Seriously. Just do it.)
✅ Put beneficiaries on your bank accounts and retirement funds.
✅ Make sure your power of attorney is up to date.

Step 3: Planning for Long-Term Care (AKA: The Part No One Thinks About Until It's Too Late)

"Alright," Penelope said. "Who here has a plan for long-term care?"

Silence.

"Yeah, that's what I thought."

✅ 70% of people over 65 will need long-term care.
✅ Medicare doesn't cover nursing homes or assisted living.
✅ A private nursing home? Easily $100,000 a year.

"So what do we do?" JJ asked.

✅ Look into long-term care insurance.
✅ Consider Medicaid planning (if needed).
✅ Start saving NOW for future healthcare costs.

Step 4: Preventing Family Drama

"You know what's worse than probate court?" Miriam asked.

"Let me guess," Carson said. "Family members fighting over money?"

"Bingo," she said.

✅ Tell your family what you want NOW. Surprises cause fights.
✅ Put sentimental items in writing.
✅ Consider a 'No-Contest Clause' in your will. (If they fight, they get nothing.)

Carl whistled. "I like that one."

The Senior Center Presentation: The Big Moment

The group realized something.

This wasn't just about money.

This was about giving their families peace of mind.

And in just a few days, they'd be standing in front of a packed senior center, teaching even more retirees how to get their affairs in order before it was too late.

Carson grinned. "So, does this make us the Estate Planning Avengers?"

JJ shook his head. "We are not calling ourselves that."

Mickey just laughed. "We are, however, calling this a win."

Final Takeaway: The Estate Planning Checklist

✅ Make a will (seriously, just do it).
✅ Get a Power of Attorney and Healthcare Directive.
✅ Talk to your family NOW, not later.
✅ Plan for long-term care before it's an emergency.
✅ Avoid probate (if possible) with a trust.

Because the best retirement plan?

Includes a plan for what comes next.

And now?

The Retirement Club was ready for their biggest challenge yet: The Senior Center Presentation.

Chapter 8: Adapting Your Playbook: The Art of Flexibility

By now, *The Last Round* felt less like a café and more like a war room.

Every week, The Retirement Club gathered, strategized, and tackled another piece of the retirement puzzle. And every week, their table grew more crowded as more retirees found their way in, clutching questions, financial anxieties, and half-baked plans.

But today's topic?

This one wasn't in any financial guidebook.

The Big Problem: Retirement Plans Fall Apart (And That's Normal)

"So," JJ said, spreading his arms. "Raise your hand if your retirement plan is going exactly as expected."

The room was silent.

Not a single hand went up.

"That's what I thought," JJ said. "Retirement plans are like New Year's resolutions—they sound great until reality slaps you in the face."

✓ Some had lost more money than expected in the market.
✓ Some had health problems that forced early retirement.
✓ Some had adult kids boomeranging back home like human-sized bills.

"So what do we do?" Linda, a retired teacher, asked. "Just… hope for the best?"

Mickey smirked. "No. We adapt."

Step 1: Reassessing Your Budget (AKA: When Plans Change, Adjust the Math)

"First," Penelope said, flipping to a fresh page in her notebook, "you have to accept that your budget isn't set in stone. It's a living thing."

✔ Unexpected medical bills? Adjust.
✔ Investment losses? Rework the numbers.
✔ Inflation eating your retirement faster than expected? Shift priorities.

"You have to treat your budget like a GPS," Penelope said. "If you hit a roadblock, you don't sit there and cry—you find another route."

Step 2: Investment Adjustments (AKA: Stop Panicking and Play the Long Game)

"Alright," Carson said, shuffling his ever-present deck of cards. "Who here freaked out when the market dipped last year?"

Several hands went up.

"Exactly," Carson said. "And who actually pulled money out of investments because of it?"

A few hesitant hands remained.

"And now?" Carson asked.

"Regretting it," one man muttered.

"Of course you are," Carson said. "Because investing is a long game. You don't win by jumping out at the first bad hand."

✅ Diversify your investments.
✅ Protect your principal without going full "stuff it under the mattress."
✅ Remember: The market has always recovered—it just takes patience.

"You panic-sell, and you lock in losses," Carson said. "You stay in the game? You have a shot at winning."

Step 3: The Side Hustle Option (AKA: Making Money Without Hating Your Life)

"Okay," JJ said, leaning in. "Let's say your plan completely falls apart."

Linda sighed. "Let's not."

"Fine," JJ said. "Let's say it… adjusts. What do you do?"

"Cut expenses?" someone offered.

"Sure," JJ said. "But you know what's even better than cutting expenses? Making more money."

✅ Freelance work? (Use skills you already have.)
✅ Consulting? (Companies still need expertise.)
✅ Renting out a spare room? (Hello, passive income.)
✅ Turning hobbies into income? (People buy weird stuff on Etsy.)

"You don't need a full-time job," JJ said. "You just need enough extra income to cover the gaps."

Step 4: The Mental Shift (AKA: Change Doesn't Mean Failure)

"You know what the real problem is?" Penelope asked.

"Other than Carson's poker addiction?" Mickey quipped.

Carson smirked. "Funny."

Penelope continued, "Most people think adjusting their plan means they failed. Like if they have to downsize or work part-time, they lost."

"Yeah," Linda admitted. "It's hard not to feel like that."

✅ Cutting expenses doesn't mean you messed up.
✅ Adjusting investments doesn't mean you failed.
✅ Taking on part-time work doesn't mean you're bad at retirement.

"It just means you're playing smart."

The Retirement Club's Eighth Rule *(Did we lose count again?)*

As they wrapped up, Penelope tapped her pen against her notebook.

"Alright," she said. "New rule:"

✅ "Retirement isn't about sticking to a plan—it's about adapting when life happens."

Mickey nodded. "That one's staying on the napkin of wisdom."

Carson grinned. "And with that, I think we just saved half this room from a financial panic attack."

JJ raised his coffee cup. "To retirement flexibility."

The room clinked glasses and coffee mugs.

Because if there was one thing The Retirement Club knew by now?

- ✔ Plans fail.
- ✔ Life changes.
- ✔ And the winners? They roll with the punches.

And now?

They were teaching others to do the same.

Chapter 9: The Home Stretch: Staying Happy, Healthy & Financially Secure

By now, The Retirement Club had figured out the mechanics of money—investments, Social Security, estate planning, all the stuff nobody ever explained properly but everyone was expected to know.

But retirement wasn't just about having enough money to survive.

It was about having enough life left to enjoy it.

And that's how today's discussion started.

Mickey set down his coffee and looked around the table. "Alright, we've spent all this time talking about how not to go broke. But what's the point if we just… sit around waiting for life to happen?"

Penelope nodded. "Retirement isn't just about finances. It's about living."

"So," Carson said, leaning forward, "how do we actually win this thing?"

Step 1: Staying Healthy (Because Money Means Nothing If You Can't Enjoy It)

"You know what's scarier than running out of money?" JJ asked.

"Running out of tequila?" Carson guessed.

"Not having the health to enjoy retirement," JJ corrected.

The table nodded in agreement. Because the truth was, you can always adjust your finances—but you can't buy a new body.

✔ Move every day – Walk, dance, lift things—preferably not just the remote.
✔ Strength training. Muscles keep you from falling like a badly stacked Jenga tower.
✔ Nutrition matters. Not saying you need to eat kale, but maybe rethink the daily cheeseburgers.
✔ Get enough sleep. Or prepare for a future where you doze off in the middle of conversations.

"So, basically," JJ said, "don't turn into a rusty old car that breaks down every five miles."

"Exactly," Penelope said.

Step 2: Staying Connected (AKA: Avoiding the #1 Retirement Killer—Loneliness)

"You know what's worse than running out of money?" Penelope asked.

"Running out of tequila?" Carson guessed again.

"Running out of people," Penelope corrected.

✔ Keep a social routine. Meet friends for coffee. Join a group. Leave the house.
✔ Talk to someone daily. Even if it's just the barista at your favorite café.
✔ Be intentional about friendships. Don't just wait for invitations—make them.
✔ Volunteer or mentor. It's scientifically proven to make you less grumpy.

"Basically," Penelope said, looking around the table, "if you want to avoid a sad, isolated retirement, stay connected."

"Or," JJ added, "get a dog."

"That too," Penelope agreed.

Step 3: Finding Purpose (Because Netflix Won't Fill the Void Forever)

"You ever meet someone who retired and just… didn't know what to do?" Betty, one of the newer attendees, asked.

Carl, a longtime member, nodded. "Yeah. That was me. The first few months were great—no alarm clocks, no deadlines. But then I woke up one day and thought, 'Now what?'"

That was the moment everyone realized:

✅ Retirement without purpose is just… existing.

Penelope pulled out her infamous notebook. "So, let's talk options."

✅ Try something new. A hobby, a skill, anything that stops you from binge-watching infomercials.
✅ Work (on your terms). Part-time, consulting, freelancing—not because you have to, but because you want to.
✅ Give back. Teach, mentor, volunteer—pass down your knowledge.
✅ Travel… but with a plan. Aimless wandering sounds fun until you realize you're just lost.

Linda, the recent widow, took a deep breath. "I never thought I'd have to figure out a new purpose at my age. But… I'm realizing it's never too late."

"Exactly," Penelope said. "We're not done yet."

One Week Until the Senior Center Presentation... And a Bigger Realization

The big moment was approaching.

In just seven days, they'd be teaching their first official retirement seminar at the senior center.

And now? They realized something:

✔ It wasn't just about finances.
✔ It wasn't just about estate planning.
✔ It wasn't even about Medicare or Social Security.

It was about LIFE.

Mickey sat back, looking around the table at this accidental movement they'd started.

"Funny," he said. "We thought we were figuring out retirement for ourselves. But we've been helping a hell of a lot of people along the way."

JJ smirked. "So… does this mean we're officially the Retirement Dream Team?"

Carson leaned in. "Guys… we're about to go pro."

And with that?

The Retirement Club prepared for their biggest moment yet.

Final Takeaway: How to Win the Final Stretch of Retirement

✅ Prioritize your health—because without it, nothing else matters.
✅ Stay connected—because isolation is the biggest retirement killer.
✅ Find purpose—because life doesn't stop when work does.

Retirement isn't just about having enough money to survive.

It's about having enough life left to enjoy it.

And now?

With one week to go until their first seminar…

The Retirement Club was ready to change lives.

Chapter 10: The Grand Finale: The Retirement Club's Senior Center Debut

The day had finally arrived.

Mickey had given boardroom presentations in his career. Penelope had lectured classrooms full of students. Carson had once given a tipsy TED Talk at a wedding about the stock market (which ended in both applause and an argument).

But this?

This was different.

The Retirement Club wasn't just talking to a handful of friends over coffee.

They were standing in front of a packed senior center auditorium, staring out at a sea of retirees who had come to hear them explain how to win at retirement.

"Alright," Mickey whispered to JJ. "Be honest. Is this terrifying?"

"More terrifying than my first mortgage," JJ muttered.

"More terrifying than realizing you accidentally hit 'reply all' on an email," Carson added.

Penelope rolled her eyes. "Oh, for goodness sake. Let's just do this."

She turned to the audience, adjusted the microphone, and smiled.

"Welcome, everyone," she said. "Let's talk about winning the retirement game."

Winning the Retirement Game: The Live Seminar

✅ Step 1: Mastering Your Finances (So You're Not Broke by 80)

Mickey stepped up. "Alright, first things first. Retirement finances are like a game of poker—you don't need to have the best hand. You just need to play smart."

Scattered chuckles. Good start.

"How many of you have a budget?" Penelope asked.

A few hands went up.

"How many of you actually follow it?"

Most hands went down.

"Exactly," Penelope said. "That's why we're here."

✅ Track your spending—because leaks sink ships.
✅ Adjust your investments—because the market changes, and so should you.
✅ Spend smart—but don't live like a hermit.

"You don't want to be the person who dies with a fortune in the bank and a fridge full of expired yogurt," Carson added.

More laughter. They were winning them over.

✅ Step 2: Planning for the Unexpected (AKA: Estate Planning & Healthcare Nightmares)

"Let's talk about what happens when life throws a curveball," Penelope said.

"Like the 2008 crash?" someone in the audience muttered.

"Like a medical emergency that wipes out your savings," Penelope corrected.

✅ Estate planning isn't just for the rich.
✅ If you don't have a will, the government decides for you.
✅ Medicare doesn't cover long-term care—so plan for it.

"You don't want your kids fighting over your furniture like a bad episode of Judge Judy," Penelope said.

Nods. Some laughter. More importantly—people were paying attention.

✅ Step 3: Actually Enjoying Retirement (Because Sitting Around Is Not a Life Plan)

"Alright," JJ said, stepping up. "We've spent all this time talking about money. But let's get real—retirement isn't just about not going broke. It's about actually living."

He looked around the room. "Who here retired and thought, 'Now what?'"

More than half the hands went up.

"See? That's the part no one prepares you for."

✅ Stay active—because your body is the only one you get.
✅ Stay connected—because loneliness is a killer.
✅ Find purpose—because sitting in front of the TV is not a retirement plan.

The Standing Ovation

As the presentation wrapped up, the audience did something none of them had expected.

They stood.

And clapped.

Loudly.

"I'll be damned," Carson whispered. "We're rock stars."

Mickey exhaled, looking at the crowd, feeling the energy in the room. This was bigger than them now.

"Alright," he said, grabbing the mic. "Same time next month?"

The crowd cheered.

And just like that…

The Retirement Club wasn't just a club anymore.

It was a movement.

Final Takeaway: The Retirement Club's Golden Rules

✅ Retirement is a game. The key to winning? Flexibility.
✅ Your money should work for you, not the other way around.
✅ Estate planning is for the living—because no one wants their family fighting in court.
✅ If you want to thrive, focus on health, purpose, and social connections.

✅ Retirement isn't just about stopping. It's about starting something new.

Epilogue: The Next Chapter

As they packed up their materials, Penelope looked around.

"We started this group just trying to figure out our own plans," she said. "But now?"

Mickey smiled. "Now, we're teaching people how to win at retirement."

JJ laughed. "Not bad for a bunch of ex-office workers and poker players."

Carson stretched. "So… celebratory drinks?"

"You mean discount happy hour?" Penelope corrected.

"Obviously."

And with that, The Retirement Club walked out of the senior center, ready to take on whatever came next.

Because retirement?

They weren't just surviving it.

They were winning it.

The End… or maybe just the beginning.

Legal Disclaimer:

This book is a work of fiction. Any similarities to real persons, living or dead, are purely coincidental.

No AI apps were harmed in the making of this book.

Maybe some nudging, but the concept, direction, style and tone were all the author's doing.

SEAN O'LEARY BOOKS

READ TO BELIEVE

Published with the wisdom and guidance of Sean O'Leary Books LLC

Visit www.seanolearybooks.com for more books by Sarai Del Mar

www.ingramcontent.com/pod-product-compliance
Lightning Source LLC
LaVergne TN
LVHW080000210926
848481LV00012B/3629
* 9 7 9 8 2 3 0 6 4 6 2 4 2 *